OUR STORY

HOW WE BECAME A FAMILY

DONOR CONCEPTION NETWORK

Text by Nina Barnsley and Stephanie Clarkson
Illustrations by Gabi Froden
Editing and Project Management by Stephanie Clarkson
Designed by Andy Archer
Produced by the 38a The Shop www.38atheshop.com
Published by the Donor Conception Network

Acknowledgements

The Donor Conception Network would like to thank the April Trust for their support in the production of these new **Our Story** books. We would also like to acknowledge Angela Mays and Jane Offord who wrote the inspirational **My Story** for sperm donation families in 1991 which was so important in helping families to be open with their children.

ISBN: 978-1-910222-95-9

Our Story 039 LCDD1

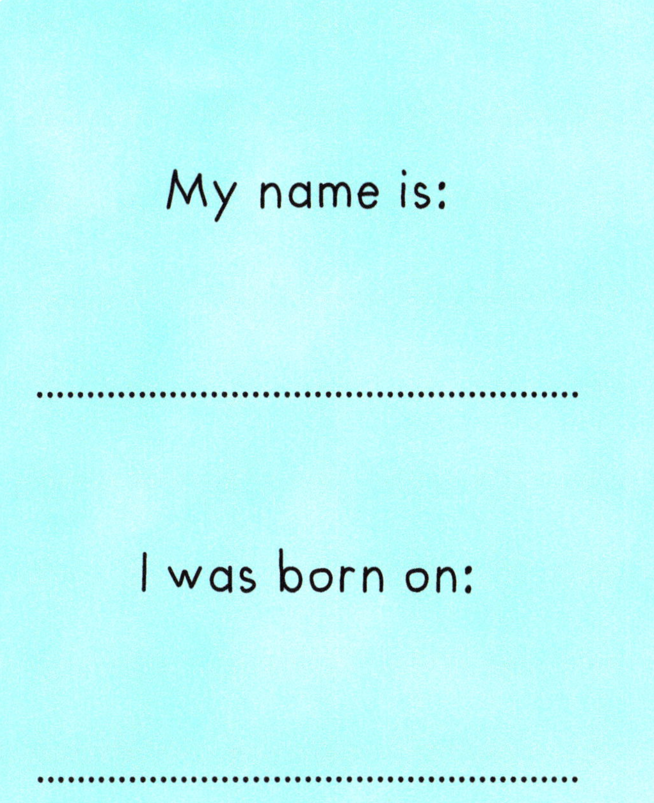

This is the story of my family.

Before I was born, Mummy and Mama
loved each other very much.

One day, they decided they wanted
a baby to love and look after.

They knew they couldn't make
a baby by themselves.

To make a baby you need a seed from
a man, an egg from a woman and a nice
warm tummy to grow the baby in.

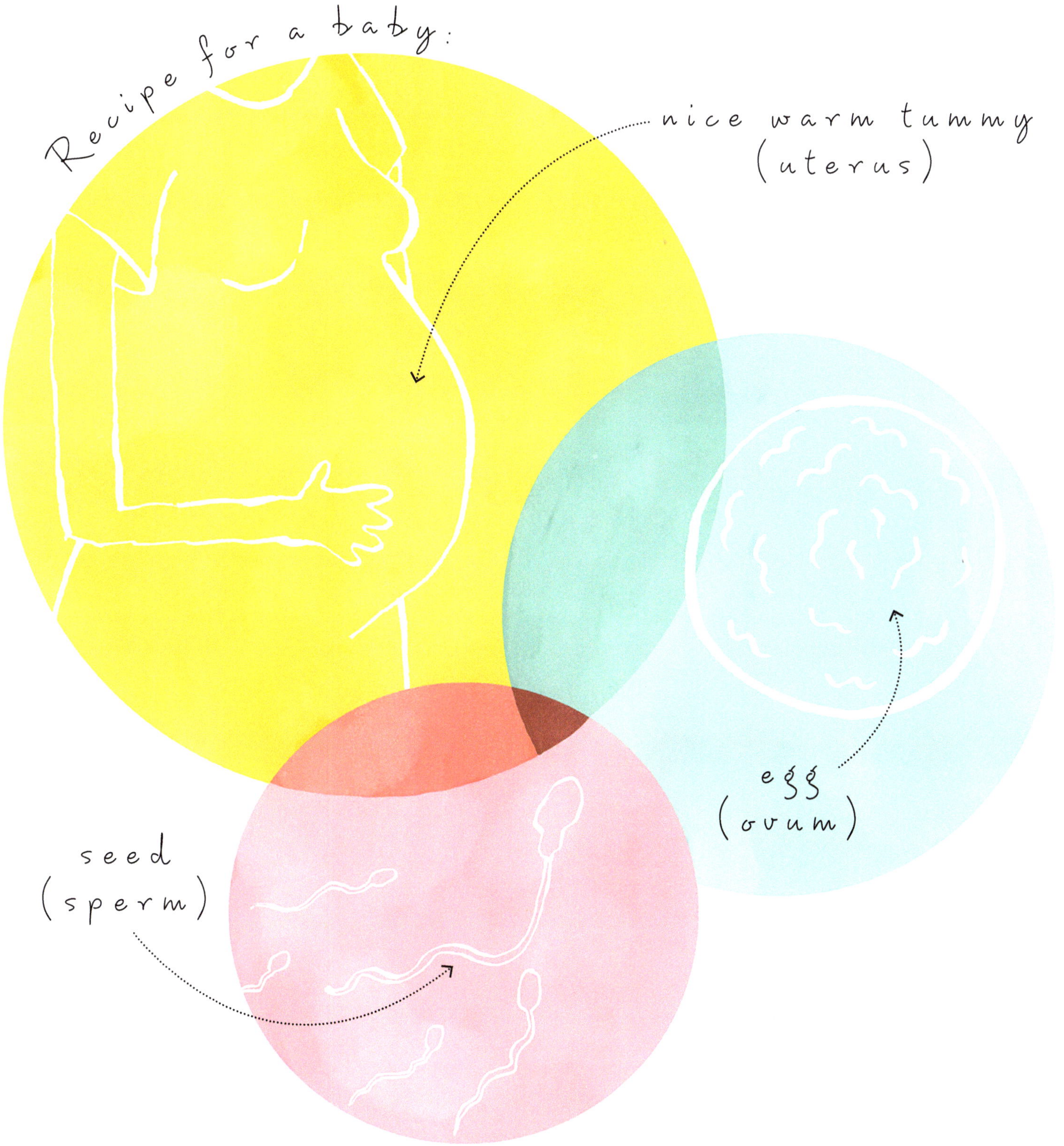

Recipe for a baby:
nice warm tummy
(uterus)
egg
(ovum)
seed
(sperm)

What could they do? Who could help?

They decided to go to see the doctor.

CLINIC

The doctor explained that there was
a way for them to have a baby, but there
were problems with Mummy's eggs so
they would need some extra help.

There are men who give some of
their seeds and women who give some
of their eggs to help other people make
a baby. They are called donors.

Lots of people choose to be donors
because they want to do something kind
and help people like Mummy and Mama
to have children.

Mummy and Mama were excited to hear
there was a way for them to have a baby.

In our family there would be no dad,
but there would be lots of love.

CLINIC

When the time was right, they went
to the clinic. The doctor put the seed
and egg from the two donors together
in Mummy's tummy.

Then they had to wait to see if
a baby would grow...

And guess what!

A baby did grow.

That baby was me!

After many months of growing
I was ready to be born.

Mummy and Mama were so pleased and
excited to meet me and hold me at last.

Family and friends came to
welcome me and say hello.

There are many different ways
that families are made and they
come in all shapes and sizes.

This is how I began and how
my family was made.

It is our story.

Here is a picture of us together.

Mummy and Mama are very proud
of our family and are so grateful to
everyone who helped make me.

Add a photo of
your family here.